Silly Animal ABCs

by Joan Gallup

COURAGE BOOKS

AN IMPRINT OF RUNNING PRESS
PHILADELPHIA • LONDON

With many thanks to Tom Crane for using his photographic skill
to give these illustrations added dimension.

© 1999 by Joan Gallup

9 8 7 6 5 4 3 2 1
Digit on the right indicates the number of this printing

Library of Congress Cataloging-in-Publication Number 98-73663
ISBN 0-7624-0506-6

Cover and interior designed by Frances J. Soo Ping Chow
Cover and interior illustrations by Joan Gallup
Typography: New Baskerville

Published by Courage Books, an imprint of
Running Press Book Publishers
125 South Twenty-second Street
Philadelphia, Pennsylvania 19103-4399

Visit us on the web!
www.runningpress.com

To the two special people in my life, Peter and Monique, and to all those I love.

is for anteater **adding up** ants.

B

is for bear in the bath
with his boat.

C

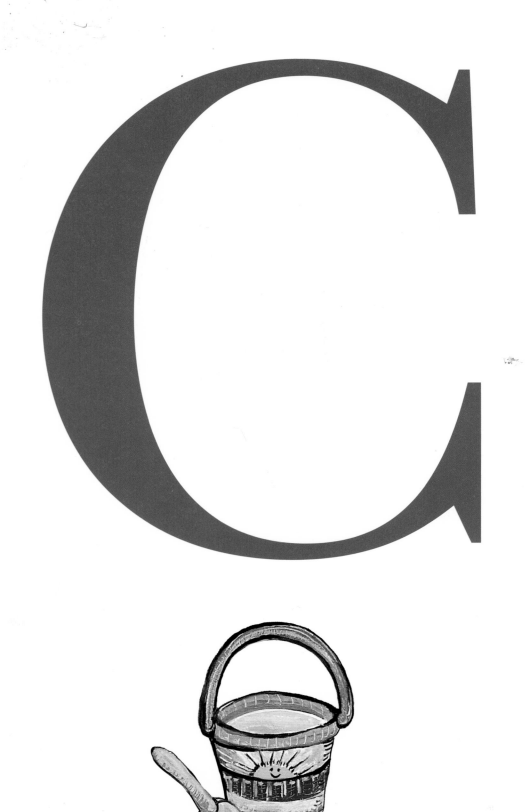

is for cat **carrying her** crabs.

is for dog **delighting**
in daffodils.

 is for elephant
eating his eggs.

is for fox
fiddling in the forest.

is for giraffe **gossiping in the** grocery.

H

is for hippo **having her** hair **done.**

is for iguana **instructing** insects.

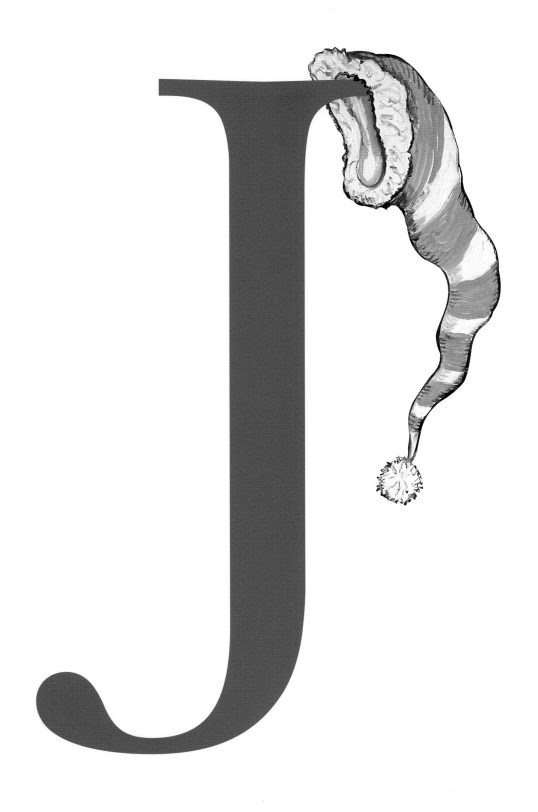

is for jaybird **jumping**
in January.

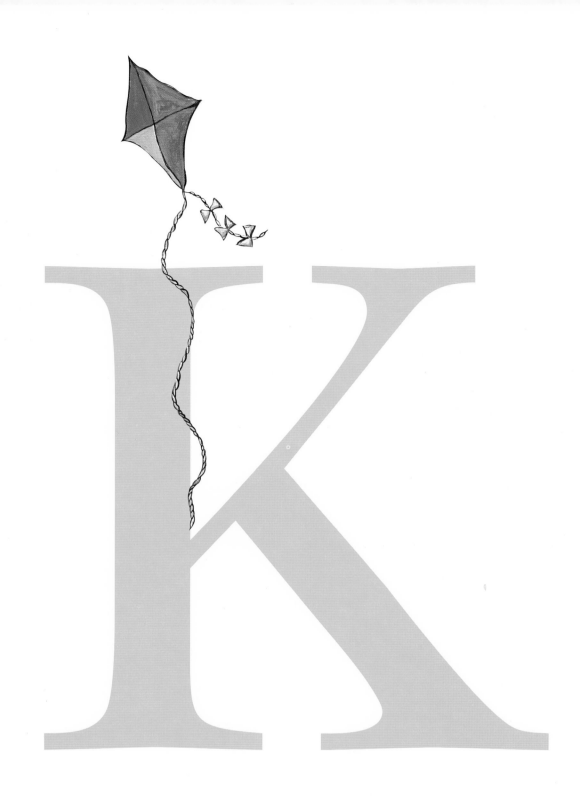

is for kangaroo

kicking his kite.

is for lion in love
with a lioness.

M

is for moose **making a** map.

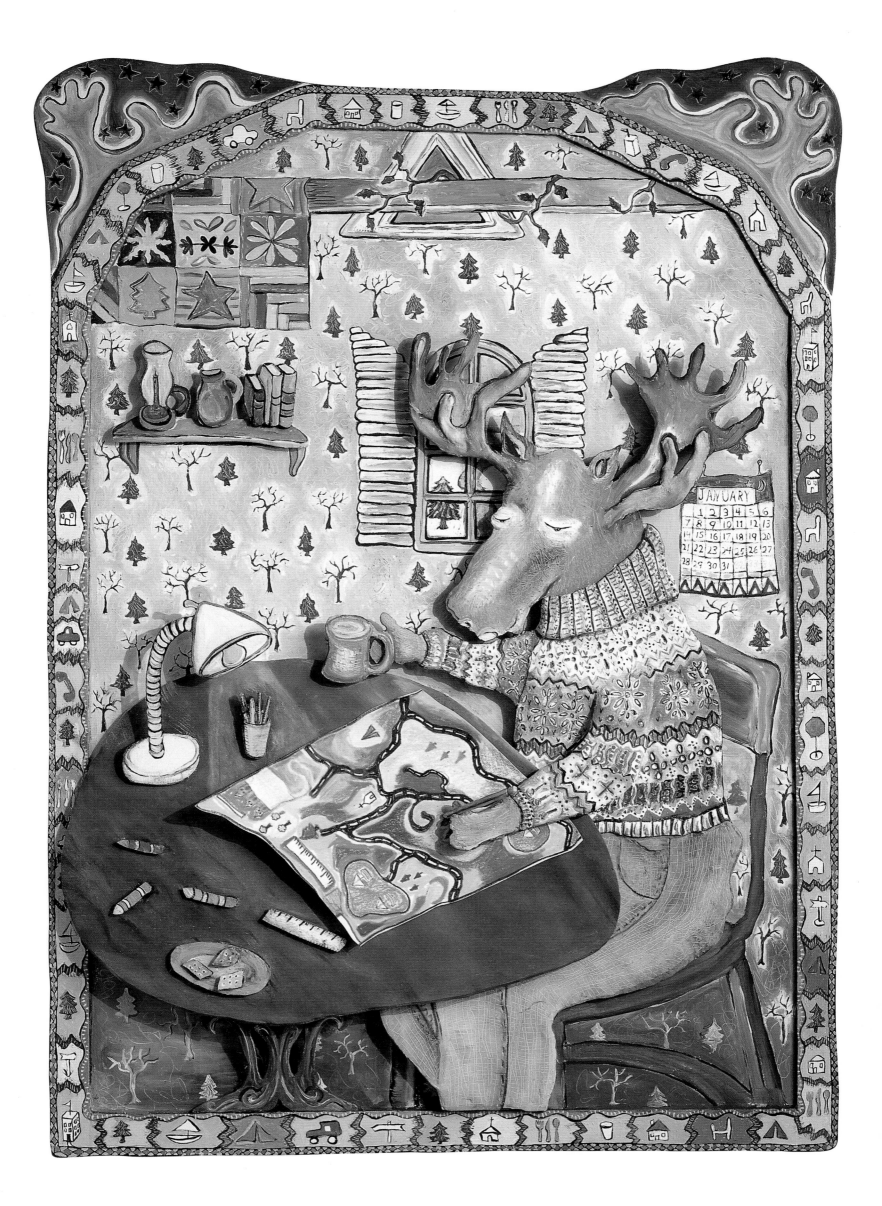

is for nightingale

now in the navy.

is for owl **at the opening**

of the opera.

P

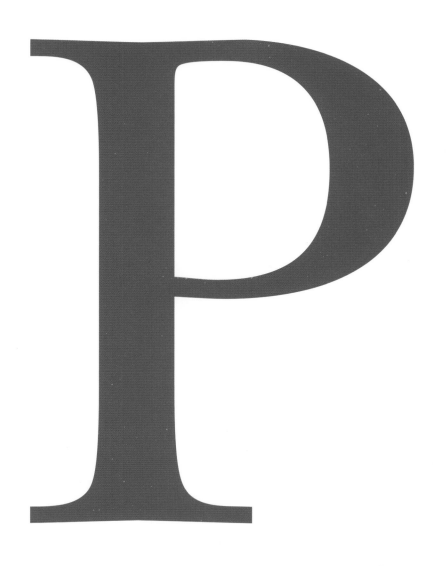

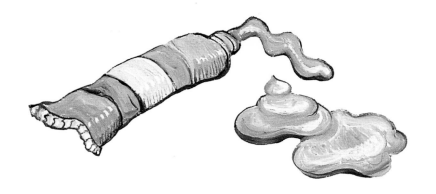

is for pig **painting a** portrait.

is for quail **quietly** quilting.

is for **rabbit** running his route.

S

is for snake **sipping her** soup.

is for tarantula **trying on** ties.

is for unicorn **under**

her umbrella.

is for vulture
on his vacation.

is for walrus **waking**

with his wife.

is for xenopus frog
at the xylophone.

Y

is for yak **out yonder in the** yard.